TARANGINI

4.

Swami Chinmayananda
and
Swamini Saradapriyananda

CENTRAL CHINMAYA MISSION TRUST

© Central Chinmaya Mission West
Total no. of copies printed between 1991 to June 2006 - 22000 copies
Revised Edition December 2011 - 3000 copies

Published by:
CENTRAL CHINMAYA MISSION TRUST
Sandeepany Sadhanalaya
Saki Vihar Road,
Mumbai - 400 072, INDIA
Tel: 91-22-28572367 / 28575806
Fax: 91-22-28573065
Email: ccmtpublications@chinmayamission.com
Website: www.chinmayamission.com

Distribution Centre in USA:
CHINMAYA MISSION WEST
Publications Division,
560 Bridgetown Pike,
Langhorne, PA 19053, USA.
Tel: (215) 396-0390
Fax: (215) 396-9710
Email: publications@chinmayamission.org
Website: www.chinmayapublications.org

Design and Illustrations
Blue Fish

Printed by Parksons Graphics

Price: ₹ 130/-

ISBN : 9788175975293

CONTENTS

Listen!
Ye Children
of
Immortal Bliss!

Mere Snapping of Fingers

Anjaneya was the greatest devotee of Lord Sri Rama and was ever ready to do whatever the Lord wished. He was prompt and active in his attentions and being a monkey could easily jump to any height or distance. He was far too quick for anyone to compete with him in serving Sri Rama. Sita, Lakshmana and his other brothers felt that Hanumana was encroaching upon their rights. One day they all came together to Sri Rama and said the duties should be properly shared and clearly defined so that no one took away any one's privilege. Sri Rama knew what was going on in their minds. He smiled and said that they should prepare a list of the duties each one was to perform.

Sita and Sri Rama's three brothers prepared

an exhaustive list of the services each one was to do. Sita was to look after the food, Lakshmana was to look after all that was needed when Sri Rama was in durbar, Bharata was to look after the raiment and clothes, and Shatrughna was to look after the weapons and the palace. No need was overlooked and no duty was omitted. Having prepared the list, they took it to Sri Rama for approval. Poor Hanumana was not allotted any duty at all. Submitting the list to Sri Rama, the four said that since the list was prepared by them all, each one should have the right to render the services listed and no one should take on the duties of another. Whenever Sri Rama needed anything he should call the person concerned and none else. Sri Rama laughingly agreed to this arrangement.

Anjaneya, who was away at the time, was later shown the list. He was told that it had been already approved by Sri Rama. Anjaneya stood in front of Sri Rama, dejected and thoughtful. How could he serve his beloved Lord now? Everything had been taken away by the others.

Sri Rama looked at him and asked, "Hanumana, do you want to say something?"

"It is about the duties, Lord," said Hanumana.

Sita and all others who were present waited for what Anjaneya would say. Would he demand the list be changed allotting him some duties also? Would Sri Rama allow it, after having already agreed to the list? To their relief, Hanumana made no such demand.

He merely said, "Lord, all the services that

can be generally rendered to you have been already allotted. Please give me the privilege of snapping my fingers whenever you yawn. Let it be my sole duty. No one else should do it."

The others laughed aloud at this request. Sri Rama hardly ever yawned and even if he did, nobody would mind Hanumana sitting in a corner and snapping his fingers. What a relief to think that hereafter they would not have to run a race with Hanumana in order to be of service to Sri Rama! Lakshmana added the duty and Hanumana's name to the list and assured him that none of them would deprive him of his privilege. But they were in for a surprise!

Hanumana's simple duty proved a greater headache for them! Now that he did not have to run about on various errands for Sri Rama, Hanumana sat at His feet, intently gazing at His face, anxious not to miss even one little yawn. Sri Rama, who was kind and considerate to all, could not bear to see the others take away Hanumana's duties. So, He kept Hanumana busy by yawning throughout the day. Whether He was in the durbar or at the palace, whether the ministers were with Him, or Sita, or His brothers, He opened his mouth wide and yawned as if He was bored with them all. Anjaneya was very happy. He was busier now than before, snapping his fingers all the time. Moreover, he was in Sri Rama's presence all day long. The brothers, and Sita were annoyed. The whole day they did not get one second alone with Sri Rama, because Hanumana was sitting there all the time.'What a nuisance!' they thought. But the worst was yet to come.

When night came, Sri Rama had his meal and retired to his room. Sita followed him after sometime, and when she was about to close the bedroom door whom did she see, but Hanumana crouching under the bed. She was horrified.

She cried out, "What are you doing here? Please leave. We have to sleep!"

Hanumana replied, "Do not worry, Mother, please go to sleep. I have to be here on duty in case the Lord yawns during the night."

Sita looked at Sri Rama helplessly. She hopefully asked Him, "Will you please allow me to do the duty of snapping my fingers during the night?"

Sri Rama looked at her and innocently said, "Dear, this morning, when you showed me the lists, all of you asked me not to let any one change duties, didn't you? How can I go against the agreement? Don't you know I am a slave to my devotees?"

Sita realised in a flash what they had done. In their selfishness they had ignored Hanumana's devotion. He had no thought except for the Lord. For the sake of the Lord, he had served them all faithfully when they were in the forest. Now that their life was easy they were keeping him out of everything. Sri Rama was teaching them a lesson through this incident.

In repentance Sita turned to Hanumana and begged his pardon. They would not come in the way of his serving the Lord. Next day when Lakshmana and the other brothers heard what happened at night, they too realised their mistake. The list of duties was thrown away, and Hanumana was happily at his place once again.

Selfishness

Once upon a time there lived a man who was a great sinner. He lied and cheated and stole from people and there was not a single living being in his village whom he had not hurt in some way. He was unrepentant and unwilling to change his ways. So when he died his record in Chitragupta's book showed only black deeds and not a single good action. He had to go to the darkest of hells.

When he was on earth he had only known how to cause pain. He never knew what it was to suffer. Now, one by one, all his past deeds gave back the sufferings which he had inflicted on others. He cried out piteously to heaven to help him escape from hell. One day, as he was praying to the Lord, a voice came from the sky, "Unfortunate man, you wish to be rescued from hell. Do you deserve it? Is there one good thing you did, which would atone your wicked deeds?"

The sinner went through his whole life on earth trying to

remember if he had done a single good deed. There was not a single act which could be considered as even tolerably good. He shook his head and woefully replied, "No, I was very ignorant then. I did not do any good action."

The voice in the sky spoke again, "Please think over it again. Perhaps there was a bad action you refrained from doing?"

The sinner again reviewed his whole life. He had cruelly hurt human beings and even animals, if they happened to cross his path. Was there any occasion when he had not done a harmful act? Suddenly he remembered. One day while walking on the road he had seen a spider crossing just in front of him. He was busy planning some mischief at the time. So he left the spider alone without killing it. Having remembered this he cried out aloud, "Yes, Lord. On one occasion, I saw a spider in front of me but did not hurt it."

"Good,"said the voice, "Then the spider can save you."

As the sinner looked at the sky, a spider appeared and wove a long web reaching from hell to the heavens. The sinner grasped the web to see how strong it was. It was strong enough to hold his weight. Happy with the thought that his delivery was near at last, he started climbing up the web. Higher and higher he went. A little more, some more.

There, almost within reach, were the heavens. Only one more heave was needed.

Just then he felt a tug below him. He looked down. Several other people in hell had also seen the web and had started to climb it. The sinner felt very angry, 'How dare they,' he thought and shouted loudly, 'Eh, you, let go of the thread. It is mine.'

The moment he said the words, the thread snapped and he fell, tumbling back straight into hell. As he fell, the voice in the sky said, 'Unfortunate one, if you cannot drop your selfishness, who can help you?'

Pride, the Bitter Enemy

Even if a man is endowed with many good qualities, just one bad quality spoils all the good ones. It is like a drop of poison in a cup of milk. All the milk is spoiled by the poison and no one dares to drink it.

Once the great Chhatrapati Shivaji was building a fort. Thousands of labourers were working for him. He gave them their due wages and being a kind man, Shivaji also arranged to provide the afternoon meal for all of them. He felt a little twinge of pride for being such a good man. His Guru, Ramadas, thought that pride should be nipped in the bud so as not to be a blemish on such a fine king.

He came to the place where the work was being supervised by Shivaji. It was lunch time and the workers were seated in long

rows to eat their food, which was brought in huge vessels. When Guru Ramadas came, Shivaji prostrated to him in great reverence. Then he stood up and pointing out the thousands of workers about to eat he said, "Guru Maharaj, I provide them with food here everyday."

The Guru sensed the pride in these words. He turned to a huge rock by the road side, examined it carefully and told Shivaji to have it broken. When the rock was broken a stream of water welled up and a small frog jumped out. Ramadas looked at the frog which had come out of the stone and said, "Shiva, did you provide food for this frog too?"

Shivaji looked at him in astonishment. "Food? For the frog?" he asked.

"Surely,"replied Ramadas, " Who else would feed it?"

In a flash Shivaji understood that he was guilty of pride. He prostrated before the teacher and gratefully said, "Thank you, Master, for putting me in my place. I shall no more be guilty of this pride."

The happy Guru smiled and blessed him. How lucky to have such a Guru who points out our mistakes the moment we are guilty of them. How lucky to be so sensible as to realise our mistakes when the Guru kindly points them out!

The Wise Minister

Once there was a king who was very, very foolish. Luckily his prime minister was very shrewd and intelligent. So the kingdom thrived and flourished.

One day the king was standing on the balcony of his palace. His minister was by his side. As the king walked, his eyes fell upon the river which was flowing through his kingdom towards the east. The king asked, "Mantriji, where does the river go, after leaving our kingdom?"

The minister replied that it flowed into the neighbouring kingdom in the east.

The king did not like this. He said, "Why should our river go into their kingdom? Put up a dam across the river and stop the water from flowing into their kingdom. We want all the water for ourselves."

The minister bowed respectfully and said, "Sire, it will be very difficult to stop the flow of the river. Moreover, we do not need so much water in our kingdom."

The king shouted, "What are you saying? Don't I know what is good for my kingdom? If there is more water, there will be more food. Go and carry out my orders."

The minister could not argue. He went and gave orders for a barrier to be raised across the river. When the natural course of the water was obstructed, it overflowed its banks and started spreading into the kingdom. All low-lying areas were soon submerged. Slowly, the level of the water rose and the whole capital was in danger of being submerged in water. Terrified people ran helter skelter to escape the danger. The representatives of the people met the minister and held a quick meeting to discuss the gravity of the situation.

The minister was in a fix. There was the king who would not listen to reason and here the people were suffering the consequences of his foolish order. How could he save the kingdom from destruction? An idea struck him. He told the representatives to keep all the people in high buildings where the water would not reach them. He promised that by morning something would be done.

Then he called the men who rang the hourly bell at night and secretly gave them some instructions. Night came. The water was slowly rising. It was two o'clock. The men rang the hourly bell - one, two, three, four, five, six! Now the king usually rose at six o' clock. He got out of bed and looked out of the window. It was still very dark and he wondered why the sun had not yet risen.

Just then the minister came running. He appeared to be in great agitation. He said, "Your Majesty, do you know what has happened? It is already six o' clock, but the sun hasn't risen and it is still dark."

The king nodded worriedly and said, "Yes, I noticed that. What is the reason, do you know?"

The minister wrung his hands helplessly and cried out, "Sire, the King of the eastern kingdom came to know that we had stopped the river from going into his kingdom. So he ordered the sun who rises in the east not to come to our kingdom. He has stopped the sun. Hereafter we will have to live in darkness. What shall we do?"

On hearing this, the king was very perturbed. How could they live without the sun? He thought deeply and said, "Mantriji, let us lift the barrier and allow the river to flow into their kingdom. Then they will allow the sun to come to us."

The minister was waiting for this. He went happily and did as he had been told. The river flowed freely and the danger to the capital was averted. By the time the barriers were lifted, it was six in the morning. The sun rose in the East. The minister came with a smile and told the king, "Look, Your Majesty, the moment we released the river, they released the sun. Now we will have plenty of sun, and enough water."

The foolish king was pleased and congratulated himself for his uncommon wisdom in allowing the river to flow!

The Three Axes

Once there lived a poor woodcutter who was honest and hard working. He went into the forest every morning to chop wood. In the evening he would sell it and earn some money. He dwelt in a small thatched hut and had an old axe with which he cut wood.

One day, he had gone to the forest as usual to chop wood. He chose a spot on the banks of a lake and started his work. Suddenly, the axe slipped from his hand and fell into the lake. It sank into the waters and disappeared. The poor woodcutter did not know how to swim. He sat by the lakeside and loudly bewailed his misfortune. His livelihood was gone and he would now have to starve.

As he was weeping, a water nymph rose from the water and asked, "My dear woodcutter, why are you weeping?" The woodcutter greeted her humbly and told her that his axe had fallen into the river and he did not know how to get it out.

The nymph suddenly disappeared into the water and came up again with a golden axe in her hands. "Is this yours?" she asked.

The woodcutter shook his head and said, "I am a poor man. Where would I get a golden axe from? It is not mine."

The nymph disappeared under the waters again and came out once more. This time she had a silver axe. Showing it to the woodcutter she asked, "Is this yours?"

The woodcutter shook his head again and said, "I am a poor man. Where would I get a silver axe?"

The nymph disappeared under the waters again and reappeared. This time she had an iron axe. "Is this yours?" she asked.

The woodcutter nodded his head in great joy and said, "Yes, it is mine. I am very indebted to you, Mother, for restoring it to me. Without this axe, I would not be able to chop wood. I would have starved."

The nymph was very pleased with his honesty. She not only gave him the iron axe but also gave the golden and silver axes as a reward for his truthfulness. The grateful woodcutter thanked her profusely and returned home. Everybody in the village came to know of his good fortune.

In the village lived another woodcutter who was very dishonest and greedy. He also wanted to become rich like the poor woodcutter. One day he picked up his axe and going into the forest reached the lakeside. He threw the axe into the lake and then started wailing loudly.

The nymph arose after a time and asked, "Why are you weeping, my good man?"

"I am a poor woodcutter earning my living by cutting and selling wood. My axe has fallen into the lake and I am unable to get it out," he replied.

Then the nymph went down into the waters and came up with a golden axe in her hand and asked, "Is this yours?"

The greedy man eagerly stretched his hand to grab it from her and cried out, "Yes, yes, it is mine. Please give it to me."

The nymph was very angry with his dishonesty and greed. "You liar, you are dishonest and greedy. Go away from here. You don't deserve any help from me." So saying she disappeared into the waters and did not come up again.

The greedy man, not only did not get the gold and silver axes, but he also lost the one good axe he had.

All is for Our Good Alone

Once a king had a minister who believed that everything happens for one's own good. No matter what happened, good or bad, he would say, 'All this is for our own good.'

One day, the king was practising fencing. By an error

of judgment the sword struck the king's little finger and it was cut off. His hand bled profusely and the doctors rushed to the spot to bandage it. The king was in great pain. He was given sedatives and as he was resting, his minister who was standing nearby, consoled the king and said, "Everything happens for the best."

The king was enraged. What silly nonsense! He was in great pain having lost a finger and here was this silly man with his stupid theory.

He shouted in anger, "Throw him into prison. Let him stay there until it is proved that losing my finger is for my own good."

The attendants came forward and arrested the minister. As they led him to the prison, the calm and unperturbed minister said, "Everything happens for the best."

In a month or two, the king's finger healed. He resumed his normal activities. One day, while he was out hunting, he got separated from his companions and got lost in a dense forest. As he was wandering around, a fierce tribal chief and his men surrounded him. The king was hopelessly outnumbered and could not fight them for long. He was bound hand and foot and taken to their temple to be offered as a sacrifice to their goddess. As they bathed his body and readied him for the sacrifice, the priest discovered that his little finger was missing. A defective person could

not be offered as a sacrifice. So the tribals took him to the edge of the forest and released him. The king returned to his palace, happy to be alive after his narrow escape.

Immediately he ordered the release of his minister. When the minister came, the king told him how he had narrowly escaped death. All because of his missing finger! He said, "My dear minister. I know now that the cutting off of my finger was for my good. But what about you? You were in prison. Was that also for your good?"

The minister smiled broadly and said, "Yes, Your Majesty, it was for my good. Had you not ordered my imprisonment, I would have surely been with you when the tribals caught you and they would have caught me too. They released you as unfit for sacrifice, but they would not have let me go because all my limbs are intact. So my life, too, was saved because I was thrown into prison."

The king appreciated his minister's wisdom and rejoiced at the ways of the Lord.

He was now convinced that God knows what to give us. When He decides to give us an experience, it is indeed always for our good.

The Bird with the Broken Wing

In a certain village there lived an old woman who though very poor was very kindhearted. One day she found a bird lying helplessly in a ditch with a broken wing. The old woman took pity on the bird and picking it up carefully took it to her hut. She bandaged the broken wing, and tenderly nursed the bird for a fortnight. The bird gradually recovered. When the wing had healed completely, the old lady set the bird free. The bird flew away fluttering its wings and the old woman was glad to see the bird so happy. After a few days the bird came to the old woman's hut, dropped a pomegranate seed in front of her and flew away.

The old woman planted the seed in her garden. By next morning, a tree had grown from the seed. On the second day, there were little red buds all over the tree. On the third day the flowers came and on the fourth day the flowers faded and tiny fruit could be seen dotting the tree. On the fifth day the fruit became bigger, and on the sixth day they were ripe. On the seventh day the old woman plucked one ripe fruit. When she cut it open, she found that it was not an ordinary pomegranate but a fruit of gold! Surprised, the old woman plucked all the fruits from the tree and saw that from within they were all made of gold. She sold the golden fruit and became very rich.

There was another old

woman in her neighbourhood. She was greedy and cruel. When she saw that the old woman had suddenly become rich, she became curious. She asked her, "How did you come by such good fortune?"

The woman told her how the bird had brought her the magic seed.

Now this old woman also wanted to get rich quickly. From that day onwards, she went about in search of a wounded bird, but a number of days passed yet she could not find one. Becoming impatient one day, she caught hold of a bird, broke its wing and carefully nursed it back to health. When the bird was well, the old woman set it free, telling it to bring her a seed by which she could get golden fruit like her neighbour. The bird fluttered its wings and flew away.

After a few days, the bird came back, carrying a seed in its beak. It dropped the seed in front of the old woman and flew away. The old woman was overjoyed. She thought that she, too, would become rich in no time like her neighbour. She took the seed and carefully planted it. The seed became a tree on the second day, brought forth flowers on the third day, fruit on the fourth day and within six days, the whole tree was full of ripe fruit. The woman plucked one fruit, took it inside, and cut it open. The moment the fruit was cut, vicious scorpions and insects crawled out of it and stung the old woman until she cried out in pain and ran away from the place!

The old woman got scorpions instead of gold because the greedy are punished by their greed itself.

A More Beautiful Pair of Eyes

In Kanchipuram there was a young man who lived an easy life. He was enamoured of a courtesan called Mohanangi and spent most of his time with her. He was especially fascinated by her lotus like eyes and he was never tired of gazing into them. In her turn, Mohanangi also dearly loved him.

Soon the chariot festival of Kanchi Varadarajaswami was to be celebrated. For this, festival crowds of pilgrims from all over India converged there and thronged the city. On the festival day, all the roads through which the chariot would pass were completely blocked by the surging crowds.

Mohanangi and her friends gathered in a street near their house with fruit and other

39

offerings for the Lord. The young man was also there, not because he was anxious to see the Lord's chariot, but because of Mohanangi. He brought an umbrella so that Mohanangi's eyes would be protected from the sun. While all the people were eagerly facing the street for the darshan, the young man stood with his back to the street holding the umbrella over Mohanangi's head and gazing into her eyes. Mohanangi felt ashamed at his behaviour. She told him to turn to the street and look at the Lord, but he could not tear himself away from her eyes.

When the Lord came, the crowd offered aarati to the deity and received the prasad. But for the young man nothing existed except his beloved.

At that time a great yogi who was there,

noticed how intently the young man was gazing into the girl's eyes, oblivious of his surroundings. He knew that such devotion was extremely rare and needed only a little push in the right direction. Walking up to the young man and patting him on the back he asked, "Son, what are you seeing?"

Without taking his eyes off Mohanangi's eyes, the young man replied, "Look, Swami, how wonderfully lovely are these eyes, I am fascinated by them."

The yogi smiled and said, "Son, there is another pair of eyes much more lovely, much more fascinating than these."

"A lovelier pair of eyes? Is it possible for a lovelier pair to exist? Where are they, Swami?" Intrigued, the young man raised his eyes from Mohanangi's face for the first time. The Swami took his arm and led him towards the Vardarajaswami temple.

They entered the temple and went up to the inner shrine. The Swami stopped in front of the deity and pointing towards it said, "There, look! Can there be a lovelier pair of eyes than these?"

The Swami's powerful personality had already stirred something deep within him and the young man stood still and looked. The beautiful, compassionate look on the Lord's face kept him rooted there. Oblivious to his surroundings he gazed at the Lord's eyes for a long time. He was no more the lustful man, but a gopi pining for the Lord's darshan. He longed to be united with the Lord and in that mood of a gopi, sang several kirtans to

the Lord asking Him to come to him. These kirtans became the famous Muvvagopala Padams of Andhra. Muvvagopala means the boy Krishna with bells on His anklets.

The devotee's name was Varadaraja.

When Can I See God?

Once there was a disciple who regularly went to a great teacher. After listening to the teacher's inspiring talks he started spiritual practice and soon came to consider himself a great sadhaka. So he would go to the teacher every day and ask him, 'O Teacher, please tell me when I will get the darshan of the Lord?'

For a few days, the teacher did not reply. He smiled and kept quiet. But the man would not stop. He continued to pester him with the same question. The teacher thought, 'What a nuisance! He must be made to understand that the Lord's darshan is not gained so cheaply.' So the next time the disciple asked his question, the teacher got up from his seat saying, "Come with me."

The disciple was pleasantly surprised. He thought that the teacher was going to show him the Lord. He followed the teacher excitedly. The teacher led him straight towards the river. The disciple followed close on his heels. The teacher entered the water and the disciple too followed. He thought that after a purificatory bath, he would get the Lord's darshan. He felt quite proud that the teacher was taking such pains for him alone, and not for the other disciples.

When they were waist deep in the water, the teacher told the disciple to take a dip. The disciple bent down and ducked his head under the water. When he was about to raise his head, the teacher caught it and kept it pressed under

the water. He did not allow the disciple to come up for a breath of air. Two or three minutes passed and the disciple felt suffocated. He writhed in agony and struggled to come up. Then the teacher let go. The disciple surfaced quickly and filled his lungs with huge gulps of fresh air.

Then the teacher asked him, "Son, when I held your head under the water, what was your foremost thought?"

The disciple said, "Teacher, what I wanted then was only fresh air. I was so restless for it. I could think of nothing else."

The teacher smiled and said,"When you are as restless for God as you were for air, you will certainly see Him!"

The Wise Choice

Once upon a time there lived a very rich man who had extensive properties and a great number of slaves. He had three sons. He died leaving a will for the disposal of his properties. After the last rites were performed, the executor of the will read it aloud in the presence of the dead man's relatives. Everyone was shocked at the contents of the will. The dead man had left all his properties including cash, houses and landed property to his favourite slave who had served him faithfully for a number of years. He made only one provision for his sons. It was mentioned in the will, that his sons might choose one item each from his properties which would be their inheritance.

The sons were stunned. Why had their

father who loved them very much, deprived them of their birthright? Why had he preferred a mere slave to his own sons? Anyway, nothing could be done about it. Their father's will was absolutely clear and they could not question it.

Each son was asked to make his choice. The eldest son chose some landed property. The second one chose a house in a business area.

Then the executor turned to the third son. "What will you choose?" he asked the young

man. The young man smiled and said, "I choose the slave to whom my father bequeathed all the properties."

The executor and all the relatives clapped in appreciation of the youngster's choice. When he chose the slave, all the property owned by the slave automatically became his. So the young man became eligible to own his father's entire estate.

Life too is like that. The Lord who created such a vast range of objects in the world, gives each one of us the chance to choose one of them. Those who choose from the objects get only that object. But he who wisely chooses the Lord Himself, becomes eligible to be the master of the whole world.

Eat When You Are Alone

One day a teacher was taking a class. The day's lesson was on God. The teacher told the students that God was present everywhere in each object and in every being. The teacher who was a great devotee explained vividly how the Lord peeped out at the world through each and every living being. The children were very impressed with the lesson and asked several questions about God. The teacher was happy to find them so enthusiastic.

The next day the teacher brought nice ripe bananas and distributed them to all the students. He told them to take the fruit to a lonely place and eat only where no one could see them.

The boys nodded and soon ran out of

the classroom. Within fifteen minutes all the children had returned except one. When questioned by the teacher, each boy said that he went to a lonely place and ate the banana.

After half an hour the last boy returned. The fruit was still in his hands. Everyone looked at him in surprise. The teacher asked the boy, "Why didn't you eat your fruit?"

The boy replied, "Sir, you told us

yesterday that God is present in all beings and peeps out at the world through them. When you asked me to eat the fruit in a lonely place where no one could see me, I ran to every nook and corner but I was never alone. Under the bushes, God looked at me through the tiny squirrels. Under the trees He looked at me through the birds. In the house, He looked at me through the ants and sparrows. When I went to the lake, He looked at me through the fishes and lotuses.

I couldn't find a place, where He was not present. Therefore I couldn't eat the fruit."

The teacher was very happy with the boy who could see God everywhere. He embraced him and said, "Son, you are correct. God watches us through all the beings. So when you have to eat or drink anything; first offer the food to Him and then eat it as His prasad."

The boy obeyed his teacher and felt very happy, because the banana tasted sweeter knowing it was the Lord's prasad.

Patience

Sant Tukarama was a great saint of Maharashtra. He was a devotee of Panduranga Viththal. Often, he was so lost in singing the glories of the Lord, that he completely forgot himself and his family. His wife Jijabai was an ordinary woman interested in material prosperity. But to her great disappointment her husband never showed any interest in amassing wealth. They were so poor that they had to go without food many a time.

Once she could no longer bear to see her children go hungry. She pleaded with Sant Tukarama and finally pursuaded him to go to the field and get some food for the children. Sant Tukarama went to the field to oblige her. There he found sticks of sugarcane, collected a bundle, put it on his shoulders and returned to the village. As he walked, he sang the praises of the Lord and quite forgot where he was going and for what purpose. He went from street to street singing the Lord's name in ecstasy. The village children, who knew his great love for everyone, came to him one by one and asked for the sugarcane sticks. Unhesitatingly, Sant Tukarama gave the sugarcane to all who asked. Then even the grownups started asking him for the sugarcane, and he gave them some as well. He did not remember his hungry children at home. By the time he reached his house, only one stick of sugarcane was left.

Jijabai came out eagerly to see what her husband had brought for the children. Only one sugarcane stick for the whole family! She was furious. In a great rage she took the stick from his hands and started

beating him with it until it broke into pieces. Sant Tukaram did not utter a single word as she beat him. When the sugarcane had broken into many pieces he smilingly said, 'Good, you have done well. Now that it is broken into pieces you can easily distribute the sugarcane to the children.'

Seeing her husband's unshakeable patience, Jijabai felt ashamed of herself.

Renunciation

Once two monks going on a pilgrimage, happened to meet on the way. Since they were both going to the same destination, they walked together. The first monk was full of praise for complete renunciation and spoke at length about its virtues. "Why need we worry about the morrow for our needs? Is not the great God who created us wise enough to provide us with what we need? He arranges the food for the smallest creature. Won't He give us what we need ?" he said.

The other monk did not completely agree with him. "True," he said, "we should depend more upon God than upon money or man, but still when we are travelling from place to place, it is not wrong to keep some money with us for emergencies."

The other monk replied that in any emergency the all knowing God Himself would certainly provide whatever was necessary.

Talking thus they came to a river. They had to cross the river in a boat. The monk who preached renunciation had no money with him. He suggested that they spend the night on the river bank singing the glories of the Lord and wait till the morning when the free ferry would start. But the second monk, who had some money with him, said it would be dangerous to spend the night in such a lonely area with wild animals roaming about. He had enough money to pay for both of them. He paid the boatman and they crossed over immediately.

Reaching the other bank, the two monks went into the village, had their food and lay down comfortably in a rest house. The monk with the money said, "This is why I feel that even a monk should keep some money

with him. Had I not got some money with me we would have been stranded there for the night, starving and exposed to all kinds of dangers. Now do you agree?"

The other monk, who believed in complete renunciation, smiled and said, "No, my friend, I am now more than ever convinced that I don't need to keep any money with me. Today I did not have any money. Who is it that sent you to be my companion and provide the boat fare for me as well? Is it not the great Lord who knows all? Why should I burden myself with an unnecessary load when He takes care of me?"

To this the second monk had no reply.

The Vanity of the Gods

Once there was a fierce fight between the gods and the demons. The demons were more powerful than the gods but the gods had the blessings of the supreme Lord on their side. So, the gods won their war. But, after it was over, they became ungrateful and forgot that their victory was thanks to the Lord. They thought vainly it was due to their own glory and power that they had won and wanted to celebrate.

The Lord knew how vain they had become. In order to teach them a lesson, He appeared in front of them in a mysterious form. The gods looked at the mysterious form but could not make out what it was.

They turned to Agnideva and asked him, "Please find out who this is."

Agni agreed to do so. He rushed towards the mysterious form. When he reached it and was about to speak, the form queried, "Who are you?"

Agni replied that he was Agni who was also known as Jataveda.

Again the form asked, "What is your power?"

Agni replied that he could burn away the three worlds.

The mysterious being put a dry blade of grass in front of him and asked him to burn it.

Agni was surprised that such a small test should be given to such a powerful being as himself. Nevertheless, he tried to burn the blade of grass. But strangely enough, all his power appeared to have left him. He tried again and again, but could not burn the grass. Defeated and dejected, he returned to the gods, unable to know who the mysterious form was.

Then the gods approached Vayudeva and asked him to find out who the visitor was. Vayu agreed and proceeded to the place where the form was standing.

Before he could start his investigation, the form asked: "Who are you?"

He said that he was Vayu, also known as Matarishwa.

The form again asked, "What is your power?"

Vayu replied that he could blow away the whole universe.

The form then placed a blade of grass before him and said, "Please blow this away."

Vayu was surprised at such an insignificant test to prove his power. However, he tried to blow it away. With all his might, he could not move the grass even a little.

Defeated and puzzled he returned to the gods, without getting to know who the form was.

Now the gods approached Indra, their king, and requested him to find out who the form was. Thus Indra set off to discover the identity of the mysterious being. But before he reached the place, the form vanished. Indra stared at the vacant space, when suddenly he saw the most graceful godess, Parvatidevi.

He asked her, "Mother, who was the visitor?"

She replied that it was the supreme Lord Himself, and said, "It was by His power that you won the battle against the demons. Forgetting that fact you claimed the glory for yourself. So He came to demonstrate the truth to you."

In an instant the gods realised their victory was that of the Lord and became humble and grateful.

Thinky Winky

(Introduction by the director of the play.)

Welcome, children. You must all be eager to see the play, and I know you will enjoy the antics and pranks of Thinky Winky. But I want you to watch carefully and see if you can find out who Thinky Winky really is. So, like a detective, watch carefully, don't forget, Thinky Winky is tricky… don't let him trick you… watch, and watch out.

(Scene One)

(A monkey enters from the right side jumping and hopping. He stops in the middle of the stage, turns towards the audience and grins.)

Monkey: Friends, do you know who I am? I am

a monkey. I am a monkey named Thinky Winky because I think. I have no eyelids but still I wink because I think. *(Sings and dances.)*

I am a monkey known as Thinky Winky I think and wink, I wink and think Thinky Winky, I am a Thinky Winky. *(Suddenly he yells in pain and stops talking. Bending down he looks at his right foot and holds it with both hands.)*

Monkey: *(face twisted in pain, moaning)* Oh, Oh, Oh... A thorn... a thorn... a crooked thorn. A thorn in my foot. I can't walk. A thorn...a thorn... a thorn... *(Cries out.)*

Barber: *(enters from the left)* Poor monkey, what happened ? Why are you weeping?

Monkey: *(weeping)* Sir, help me, help me. A cruel thorn has pierced my foot and gives me endless pain. Help me Sir, show pity upon a helpless, hapless, miserable monkey!

Barber: Sure, I shall do my best. Let me see your foot. *(Puts his case on the ground, sits down and examines the foot.)* Ah, there! The cruel thorn has gone right into the foot. Wait, a minute. *(Opens his case and takes out a knife. With its sharp tip, he pulls out the thorn.)* See, this is the thorn that hurt you so much. Now you are rid of it. Go and be happy. *(Breaks the thorn and throws it away. Then he takes up his case and rises to go.)*

Monkey: *(joyfully)* Ha, Ha, Ha! I am happy. I am very very happy. The pain is gone. Thank you so much, Sir. I will never forget you. *(The barber smiles and goes on his way. The monkey runs behind him.)*

Monkey: Sir, Sir, where is my thorn? You are going away without giving me my thorn. You ought not to rob a poor monkey. Please give me back my thorn.

Barber: *(surprised)* Thorn? Why do you want the thorn? I broke it and threw it away.

Monkey: What? You broke my nice precious thorn. You threw it away? *(in anger)* What right have you, Sir, to break my thorn? What right have you to throw it away? No, I want it. I must have it. You must get it back for me. My precious thorn! My invaluable thorn! Why did you pull it out? Had you not pulled it out, it would have remained with me. My darling thorn would have remained with me.

Barber: Go away you silly thing. The thorn is broken. It can't come back. If you want one, pick another one. There are plenty of them here. *(He brushes the monkey aside and tries to go.)*

Monkey: What do you mean, 'Get another thorn?' If your son gets lost, will you take another man's son? How can I take another thorn? I want my own thorn. My own pretty thorn! Give it to me.

Barber: *(in disgust)* If you want your own pretty thorn, sit and weep. It is gone forever. It will not come back.

Monkey: *(obstructing the barber)* If the thorn can't come back to me, then your knife can. Your knife pulled out the thorn, otherwise my beautiful thorn would have been with me. Give me the knife...the knife or thorn...thorn or knife...knife or thorn. *(Obstructs the barber who tries hard to escape but in vain.)*

Barber: *(dismayed)* What a wretched monkey you are! Most unreasonable. I took pity upon you and helped you. This is how you repay me. It was my mistake. I ought to have left you yelling and wailing in pain, I was such a fool. *(Takes out the knife from his case, throws it before the monkey and goes away. The monkey grins and winks at the audience as he picks up the knife.)*

(The curtain falls.)

(Scene Two)

(The monkey enters carrying the knife on his shoulder like a sword, singing and dancing.)

Monkey: I am a monkey known as Thinky Winky. I think and wink, I wink and think Thinky Winky, I am Thinky! By thinking I got rid of the thorn. By winking I got a knife in return!

(He sees a woodcutter cutting firewood. The woodcutter is unable to cut the wood well and is muttering under his breath.)

Monkey: *(drawing near him)* Dear Sir, why do you curse the firewood?

Woodcutter: *(looking up at the monkey)* No, I am not cursing the firewood. I am cursing my own bad luck. My axe is blunt and does not go through the wood. If I can't cut this wood by noon there will be no money and my family at home will have to starve.

Monkey: My poor woodcutter! I am sorry for you. Let me help you. Here, take this knife. It is very sharp.

Woodcutter: *(taking the knife in great joy)* What good luck! Thank you very much, dear monkey. I am greatly indebted to you. *(Starts cutting with the knife. The monkey stands nearby and looks on. After a time the knife breaks)* Alas, the knife is broken!

Monkey: *(running near)* Why, what happened? Why are you crying ? *(Sees the broken knife.)* You wretch you broke my knife. You broke my wonderful powerful knife. Why did you break it ? What made you break it ?

Woodcutter: I am so sorry, monkey. I did not break the knife. It was a thin one. It broke by itself. Believe me, I did not do it deliberately. *(Bundles up the firewood, puts it on his head and prepares to leave.)*

Monkey: *(mimicking the woodcutter)* I did not do it deliberately! Then how did it break ? It deliberately broke itself, I suppose. Give back my knife to me. Give me my knife or else give me the wood that broke it. I will not allow you to escape. *(Whichever way the woodcutter tries to escape, the monkey hops and jumps and prevents him from going.)*

Woodcutter: *(angrily)* What an obstinate monkey you are! I thought you were kind and considerate. Can't you see that the knife broke of its own accord? I ought not to have accepted your help. I have been such a fool. *(Throws down*

the firewood and escapes. The monkey grins and winks as he picks up the firewood from the ground.)

(The curtain falls.)

(Scene Three)

(The monkey enters with the firewood on his head, singing and dancing.)

Monkey: I am a monkey known as Thinky Winky.

I think and wink, I wink and think. Hence I am known as Thinky Winky. By thinking I got rid of the thorn and got a wonderful knife instead. By thinking I gave the knife to a man. And got the firewood instead.

(Stops on seeing an old woman making dosas. The woman is fanning the oven very hard but no flames come out because there is not much fuel in the oven.)

Woman: *(fanning the oven and muttering to herself)* No use. No use at all.

Monkey: *(drawing near)* Dear Granny, why do you keep saying 'No use', 'No use', 'No use'? Don't you like to make dosas ?

Woman: I do like to make dosas. But what can I do? There is no firewood in the oven and it is cold. Good dosas cannot be made without fire.

Monkey: My poor Granny. How I pity you! Let me help you. Here, take this firewood. *(Gives her the bundle on his head.)*

Woman: *(beaming with joy)* How kind you are! Thank you very much. *(Takes the firewood and puts it in the oven. Soon there is a nice blaze. A merry fire crackles and hot dosas are quickly made. The woman makes a neat packet of the dosas and gets up to go.)* Many many thanks, my little monkey. I shall never forget you in my life. *(The monkey jumps up and obstructs her. The old woman is startled by the sudden jump.)*

Monkey: *(mimicking the woman)* Many many thanks, my little monkey. Thanks indeed! What sort of thanks are they? You run away like a thief without returning my firewood. Give me back my firewood.

Woman: *(surprised)* What do you mean ? You gave me the fuel yourself. I did not ask for it. It is all burnt to make dosas. How can it come back again ?

Monkey: I don't know all that. What I want is my firewood. Give it back to me and then leave. At your age, you cheat a poor monkey like me ? If the firewood is burnt up to make the dosas, then give me the dosas instead. I won't allow you to go unless you give me either of them. A nice way of cheating this is! *(The old woman tries to escape. Whichever way she turns the monkey jumps in front of her.)*

Woman: *(weeping angrily)* What a naughty monkey you are! I thought you took pity on me and helped me. I was such a fool to believe you. Take them all, you rascal ! *(Throws the packet of dosas in front of the monkey and escapes.*

The monkey winks at the audience and picks up the packet with a grin.)

(The curtain falls)

(Scene Four)

(The monkey enters carrying the packet of dosas like a ladies' hand bag.)

Monkey: I am a monkey known as Thinky Winky. I think and wink, I wink and think. Hence am I known as Thinky Winky. By thinking I got rid of a thorn. And got a wonderful knife instead. By thinking I gave the knife to a man and got the firewood instead. By thinking I gave the firewood and got a packet of dosas instead.

(Sees a drummer proclaiming in a feeble voice which is hardly audible. He looks weak and emaciated.)

Drummer: *(weakly beating his drum)* I hereby make it known to one and all *(voice dies away.)* Alas, what am I to do now? I can't manage. *(Sighs and wipes his face.)*

Monkey: *(going near)* Drummer, why are you murmuring your proclamation? Your voice is not audible at all. Why don't you speak loudly? How, will people know what you are proclaiming ?

Drummer: *(feebly)* What can I do, monkey. For the last three days, I have not had any food. I can hardly stand. I am too weak to even hold this drum. I am very hungry.

Monkey: My poor drummer, my heart bleeds for you. Let me help you. Here take this packet. There are plenty of dosas in it. *(Gives the packet.)*

Drummer: *(receiving it in great glee)* I never dreamt of this. Thank you very much, my dear monkey. How nice of you to take pity upon a miserable man. May the Lord bless you ! *(Opens the packet and eagerly eats all the dosas. He throws away the empty paper packet and taking up his drum starts beating it vigorously.)* It is hereby made known to one and all… *(His voice rings out loud and clear. He moves on, proclaiming loudly, when suddenly the monkey comes from behind and obstructs his way.)*

Drummer: *(bewildered)* Why do you come in my way? Let me go. I am already late. I have to finish the whole area before evening.

Monkey: *(mocking him)* You have to finish the whole area before evening, do you? What about my dosas? Return them and start your work.

Drummer: *(surprised)* What are you saying?

I ate all the dosas. You gave them to me! Don't play monkey tricks on me. *(He tries to leave. Whichever way he turns, the monkey leaps and jumps, coming in his way.)*

Monkey: You are most ungrateful. You eat all my dosas and run away like a thief. Give me back my dosas, or else, this drum, or I won't allow you to go. *(Lays his hands on the drum firmly and prevents the man from moving.)*

Drummer: *(shouts angrily)* What a crooked monkey you are ! I thought you were a nice kind monkey. You are a devil incarnate. I was a fool not to have known you better. Have it your own way. *(Throws down the drum with a bang and escapes.)*

Monkey: *(Takes up the drum with a grin and starts singing and dancing while beating on the drum.)* I am a monkey known as Thinky Winky.

I think and wink, I wink and think hence I am known as Thinky Winky. The dosas are gone but the drum is mine. All the while the benefit is mine and mine alone.

(Turning to the audience) Good bye friends! Don't ever try to beat me at my game. Me, the Monkey-Winky, none can outwit, nor ever defeat. Avoid me if you can. At a distance you are safe. *(Gives a big grin and jumps off the stage.)*

(The curtain falls)

Director of the play:

Now, children, the play is finished and I hope you all had a good time and enjoyed it thoroughly. Did you remember the warning I gave you in the beginning? Do you know who Thinky Winky is? Yes, I think you know this monkey who is weeping and grinning, hopping and jumping. He is like your mind. Now happy, now sad, full of mischief, full of tricks. Thinky Winky drove a good bargain. From a thorn in his foot he worked himself up to be the owner of all those dosas. So, too, the mind can help us to reach higher but, beware, it is full of tricks, and it can also pull us down. Thinky Winky cheated, all for a few dosas! Those will soon be eaten. Then what? No real wealth can be earned by cheating. What is gained by the mind may be lost by it. The mind is an instrument that must be used properly, not to gain anything that can be lost, but to gain something else. Watch and see if you can find it.

Verses to Learn

पतितोऽपि कराघातैरुत्पतत्येव कन्दुकः।
प्रायेण साधुवृत्तानामस्थायिन्यो विपत्तयः॥

patito'pi karāghātairutpatatyeva kandukaḥ,
prāyeṇa sādhuvṛttānāmasthāyinyo vipattayaḥ.

A ball, dashed to the ground with the hand,
bounces up again. So too, the downfall of good
men does not last long.

आलस्यं हि मनुष्याणां शरीरस्थो महान् रिपुः।
नास्त्युद्यमसमो बन्धुर्यं कृत्वा नावसीदति॥

ālasyaṁ hi manuṣyāṇāṁ śarīrastho mahān ripuḥ,
nāstyudyamasamo bandhuryaṁ kṛtvā nāvasīdati.

Laziness is the greatest enemy of man. Work
(activity) is his best friend, finding which, he will
never sustain a loss.

श्लोकार्धेन प्रवक्ष्यामि यदुक्तं ग्रन्थकोटिभिः।
परोपकारः पुण्याय पापाय परपीडनम्॥

ślokārdhena pravakṣyāmi yaduktaṁ granthakoṭibhiḥ,
paropakāraḥ puṇyāya pāpāya parapīḍanam.

In half a shloka I will tell you all that has been
said in crores of scriptures: doing good to others
is virtue; troubling them is sin.

80

पद्माकरं दिनकरो विकचीकरोति
चन्द्रो विकासयति कैरवचक्रवालम्।
नाभ्यर्थितो जलधरोऽपि जलं ददाति
सन्तः स्वयं परहितेषु कृताभियोगाः॥

padmākaraṁ dinakaro vikacīkaroti
candro vikāsayati kairavacakravālam,
nābhyarthito jaladharo'pi jalaṁ dadāti
santaḥ svayaṁ parahiteṣu kṛtābhiyogāḥ.

The sun, by itself, opens the lotus buds; the moon unasked, opens the kumud clusters; unasked, the clouds give rain; so too, the good, unasked, are anxious to benefit the world.

Code of Conduct for the Chinmaya Mission Members

Chinmaya Mission members should:

- Try to live up to and fulfil the motto as well as the pledge of the Mission.

- Daily spare time for meditation and scriptural study.

- Once a week, on a convenient day offer prayers at a nearby temple with members of their family.

- Discover a life of harmony at home and on no account create any domestic unhappiness.

- Have satsanga at home with the children and other family members. Reading of the Ramayana, Mahabharata and Bhagavat Mahapurana in a language familiar to the children would be an important part of the programme.

- Greet other Mission members with 'Hari Om'.

- Inculcate the practice of daily offering pranams to the elders in the house.

Chinmaya Mission Pledge

We stand as one family
bound to each other with love and respect.

We serve as an army
courageous and disciplined,
ever ready to fight against
all low tendencies and false values,
within and without us.

We live honestly
the noble life of sacrifice and service,
producing more than what we consume,
and giving more than what we take.

We seek the Lord's grace
to keep us on the path of virtue, courage and
wisdom.

May Thy grace and blessings
flow through us to the world around us.

We believe that the service of our country
is the service of the Lord of Lords,
and devotion to the people
is the devotion to the supreme Self.

We know our responsibilities,
give us the ability and courage
to fulfil them.

Om Tat Sat